Tng

Drums

A & C Black • London

Published 2000 by A & C Black (Publishers) Ltd
35 Bedford Row, London WC1R 4JH

Copyright © 2000 A & C Black (Publishers) Ltd

ISBN 0-7136-5397-3

A CIP catalogue for this book is available from
the British Library.

Printed and bound in the UK by The Cromwell Press,
Trowbridge, Wiltshire.

Contents

Death

Pride and Defiance

The Changing Times

Introduction

Dear Reader,

Let me tell you a secret: this selection of poems is in fact a story, the story of Africa as told by some of its very best poets.

The anthology is divided into seven parts. The first one is about the universe, nature and the way man fits into all this. The second part talks about animals, their beauty, their special traits. Then comes 'Love and Celebrations', because love in all its aspects will always remain the most important thing in life. Without love, there is no happiness. The fourth section is about people, what they do, who they are and how they see life. But there is also death, the theme of the fifth section, which is part of life. Death is approached in different ways by the poets.

The sixth section, 'Pride and Defiance', is mainly dedicated to the *Négritude* movement. The struggle for independence from colonial rule articulated the demands of African people in a literary language that promoted cultural identity and pride. Léopold Sédar Senghor from Senegal was one of the founders of this movement together with Aimé Césaire and Léon Gontran Damas, the poets from the French West Indies. The period of the *Négritude* followed the Black Renaissance in America and was greatly influenced by its promotion of Black culture. The feelings of disillusionment that can be read in some of the pieces in the next section, 'The Changing Times', come as a reaction to the turmoil which has shaken many African countries. The economic hardship, dictatorial government and military regimes that followed the euphoria of the Independence have caused discontent.

The white colonial is no longer identified as the sole figure of oppression, even though the past still weighs heavily upon the continent. Africans are critical of their own governments in their desire for democracy and progress. As a consequence of this criticism, some poets have been imprisoned, or forced to leave their homes. Others have been killed in conflict. Christopher Okigbo, the Nigerian poet, died fighting in the Biafran civil war. Ken Saro Wiwa, from the same country, was put to death by the military government a few years ago. The many new poets who feature in this section are the voices of contemporary Africa and the themes they choose to write on are as diverse as they are universal. Many of these poets are well travelled and speak as citizens of the world.

Almost everywhere in Africa, traditions are dying out. Abidjan, Dakar and Lagos in the west, Johannesburg in the south, Nairobi in the east and Kinshasa in the centre, are cosmopolitan cities where the demands of urban life leave very little room for past customs and practices, good or bad. Moreover, cultural influences from western countries are strongly felt throughout the media, the cinema, literature and fashion. This is why it is so important to give traditional oral poetry its rightful place in this selection of poems. Indeed, oral poetry existed well before the arrival of Arabs and Europeans on the continent. It was part of the oral literary tradition and was composed in indigenous African languages.

Poetry was once so common in African life that almost nothing was done without it. During royal and religious ceremonies professional singers, or griots, composed songs to praise the king and the gods. Domestic ceremonies like weddings, funerals, births, initiation rites and harvest festivals, were all performed to the accompaniment of poetry. Poetry in the oral tradition followed the ancient way of eloquence and rhythm and was passed down the generations. Much research is still needed to recover the identity of those who created these beautiful poems which are in many ways very modern in their approach to universal themes.

For several centuries millions of Africans were forcibly shipped as slaves to the Americas. More recently, a great number went to Europe as workers. They stayed on and today their children and grandchildren are now European citizens in the same way that Blacks in the United States are American citizens. Exile is a common theme in the final section. You will also feel the strong presence of women poets throughout this selection of poems, as contemporary poetry has seen the emergence of new, strong feminine voices. Although in the past women had a key role in the transmission of oral literature through storytelling and poetry, their influence and contribution have not been entirely acknowledged and it is only in these last decades that they have really been able to establish themselves.

Happiness and sorrow, life and death, anger and humour, disillusion and hope, it is all here. You will recognize yourself in the many emotions expressed by the poets. I hope that this introduction to African poetry will lead to further readings and maybe even spark off a passion for the poetry which means so much to me personally.

Véronique Tadjo

Our Universe

Hymn to the Sun

The fearful night sinks
trembling into the depth
before your lightning eye
and the rapid arrows
from your fiery quiver.
With sparking blows of light
you tear her cloak
the black cloak lined with fire
and studded with gleaming stars –
with sparking blows of light
you tear the black cloak.

Traditional, Fang

Invocation to the Rainbow

Rainbow, O Rainbow,
You who shine away up there, so high,
Above the forest that is so vast,
Among the black clouds,
Dividing the dark sky,

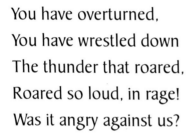

You have overturned,
You have wrestled down
The thunder that roared,
Roared so loud, in rage!
Was it angry against us?

Among the black clouds,
Dividing the dark sky,
As a knife cuts through an over-ripe fruit,
Rainbow, Rainbow!

And it fled,
The thunder killer of men,
Like the antelope from the panther,
Rainbow, Rainbow!

Strong bow of the Hunter above,
The Hunter who hunts down the herd of the clouds
Like a herd of elephants in terror,
Rainbow, speak our thanks to him
Say to him: 'Be not angry!'
Say to him: 'Be not wrathful!'
Say to him: 'Kill us not!'
For we are greatly afraid,
Rainbow, tell him so!

Traditional, Pygmy (Cameroon/Gabon)

The Sky

The sky at night is like a big city
Where beast and men abound,
But never once has anyone
Killed a fowl or a goat,
And no bear has ever killed a prey.
There are no accidents; there are no losses.
Everything knows its way.

Traditional, Ewe (Ghana)

Who Knows?

Who knows
How many stars
Are in the roof of the sky?
How many fishes
In the deep seas?
How many people
In the whole wide world?
Who knows
Where, every evening
The sun flees to?
Where the moon lights up?
Where dawn starts,
Where the endless horizon ends,
Who knows?... Who knows?

Fatou Ndiaye Sow (Senegal)

Mawu of the Waters

I am Mawu of the Waters.
With mountains as my footstool
And stars in my curls
I reach down to reap the waters with my fingers
And look! I cup lakes in my palms.
I fling oceans around me like a shawl
And am transformed
Into a waterfall.
Springs flow through me
And spill rivers at my feet
As fresh streams surge
To make seas.

Abena P. A. Busia (Ghana)

But Sometimes When it Rains

But sometimes when it rains
and an angry thunder raps earth's ears
with its hands of fire
sometimes when it rains
and a heartless storm beheads
the poor man's house
like some long-convicted felon

    Sometimes when it rains
    you wonder who sent the skies weeping

Sometimes when it rains
and an impregnable mahogany falls
across your farmyard path
sometimes when it rains
and a streamlet swollen with watery pride
drowns your fields and tender tubers

    Sometimes when it rains
    you wonder who sent the skies weeping

Sometimes when it rains
and a diligent tryst is washed out
by a careless downpour
sometimes when it rains
and a callous mist thickens
between you and the waiting one
sometimes when it rains
dreams are wet with the desperate longing
of jilted embrace
You wonder who sent the skies weeping
sometimes when it rains

Niyi Osundare (Nigeria)

On the Island

When the rain came
It came in a quick moving squall
Moving across the island
Murmuring from afar
Then drumming on the roof
Then marching fading away

Dennis Brutus (South Africa)

The Key

My child, my hope,
Everything in nature
Speaks to you:
The sun, the moon
The bird
Which flies by
The river which flows
And even the cold stone;
If you know
How to listen, look and feel,
You will find the key to the universe.

Fatou Ndiaye Sow (Senegal)

The Animal Kingdom

The Lion

The lion has a golden mane,
A golden coat
And golden eyes.

The gazelle leaps across the plain,
And seems to float,
Across the skies.

Uzo Nwokedi (Nigeria)

Extract from

The Lion Roars with a Fearful Sound

The lion roars with a fearful sound,
   Roar, roar, roar!

The lion creeps, its prey to catch,
   Creep, creep, creep!

The lion pounces with a mighty leap,
   Leap, leap, leap!

The lion eats with a crunching sound,
   Crunch, crunch, crunch!

The lion sleeps with a gentle snore,
   Snore, snore, snore!

Mabel Segun (Nigeria)

Song of the Lioness for her Cub

Fear the one
who has sharp weapons
who wears a tassel of leopard tail,
he who has white dogs –
O son of the short-haired lioness!
My short-eared child,
son of the lioness who devours raw flesh,
You flesh-eater!
Son of the lioness whose nostrils are red with
   the bleeding prey,
you with the bloodred nostrils!
son of the lioness who drinks water from the swamps,
You water-drinker!

Traditional, Hottentot

Kob Antelope

A creature to pet and spoil
An animal with a smooth neck.
You live in the bush without getting lean.
You are plump like a newly-wedded wife.
You have more brass rings round your neck
than any woman.

When you run you spread fine dust
like a butterfly shaking its wings.
You are beautiful like carved wood.
Your eyes are gentle like a dove's.
Your neck seems long, long
to the covetous eyes of the hunter.

Traditional, Yoruba (Nigeria)

A Baby Antelope

A baby antelope
Once asked her pensive mother:
    Tell me mother
    How does one count the teeth of a lion?

Niyi Osundare (Nigeria)

Mother Parrot's Advice to her Children

Never get up till the sun gets up,
Or the mists will give you a cold,
And a parrot whose lungs have once been touched
Will never live to be old.

Never eat plums that are not quite ripe,
For perhaps they will give you a pain;
And never dispute what the hornbill says,
Or, you'll never dispute again.

Never despise the power of speech;
Learn every word as it comes,
For this is the pride of the parrot race,
That it speaks in a thousand tongues.

Never stay up when the sun goes down,
But sleep in your own bed,
And if you've been good, as a parrot should,
You will dream that your tail is red.

Traditional, Ganda, A.K. Nyabongo

Extract from

The Magnificent Bull

My bull is white like the silver fish in the river
white like the shimmering crane bird on the river bank
white like fresh milk!
His roar is like the thunder to the Turkish
  cannon on the steep shore.
My bull is dark like the raincloud in the storm.
He is like summer and winter.
Half of him is dark like a storm cloud,
half of him is light like sunshine.
His back shines like the morning star.
His brow is red like the beak of the Hornbill.
His forehead is like a flag, calling the people from a distance,
He resembles the rainbow.

Traditional, Dinka

Song of the Animal World

The fish goes...   Hip!
The bird goes...   Viss!
The monkey goes...   Gnan!

I start to the left,
I twist to the right,
I am the fish
That slips through the water,
That slides,
That twists,
That leaps!

Everything lives,
Everything dances,
Everything sings:
The fish goes...   Hip!
The bird goes...   Viss!
The monkey goes...   Gnan!

The bird flies away,
Flies, flies, flies,
Goes, returns, passes,
Climbs, floats, swoops.
I am the bird!

Everything lives,
Everything dances,
Everything sings:
The fish goes...   Hip!
The bird goes...   Viss!
The monkey goes...   Gnan!

The monkey! From branch to
          branch
Runs, hops, jumps,
With his wife and baby,
Mouth stuffed full, tail in air,
Here's the monkey! Here's the
          Monkey!

Everything lives,
Everything dances,
Everything sings:
The fish goes...   Hip!
The bird goes...   Viss!
The monkey goes...   Gnan!

Traditional (Zaire/Democratic Republic of Congo)

Crab

Crab with a small brain
Why do you
Go backward
To go forward?
Is it my own world
Is it your own world
Which is upside down?
Lucky you are not a car
Otherwise,
Oh dear, oh dear,
You would have so many accidents!

Irene Assiba D'Almeida (Benin Republic)

The Free Bird

The bird who passes over there
The light bird
Who flaps his wings
And slices through the air over there in the horizon,
Doesn't own a thing in the world,
But how freedom
Makes him pretty!

And he lives singing
On the branch
This beautiful travelling bird
Who gives rhythm to the seasons

For nothing is worth freedom:
It is the most dignified of all fortunes
The freedom which the bird
Who lives on the branch enjoys!

Freedom and its sacred fire
Natural freedom
O sacred freedom
Which should be enjoyed
By any being
In his simple state!

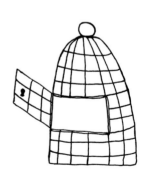

Claude-Joseph M'bafou-Zetebeg (Cameroon)

Love and Celebrations

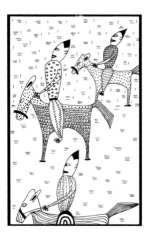

Love-song

All things in nature love each other:
The lips love the teeth,
The beard loves the chin,
And all the little insects go brrrrr together.

Traditional (Soga)

A Heart

A heart to hate you
Is as far as the moon.
A heart to love you
Is near as the door.

Traditional (Burundi)

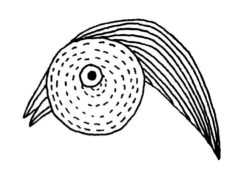

My House

I have built my house
Without sand, without water
My mother's heart
Forms a great wall
My father's arms
The floor and the roof
My sister's laughter
The doors and the windows
My brother's eyes
Light up the house
My home feels good
My home is sweet

Annette Mbaye d'Erneville (Senegal)

As Soon as Night Falls

As soon as night falls
As soon as the soft moon appears
Child,
Think about your mother.

As soon as the stars are born in thousands,
As soon as the cicadas sing festively,
Child
Think about your mother.

As soon as your keen sense of hearing
Catches the frightening call of the owl,
Little child
Think about your mother.

As soon as fear grabs hold of you,
As soon as anguish fills your innocent heart,
Cry no more, little one
Cry no more
But think about your mother.

As soon as hunger troubles your weak eyes,
As soon as your frail legs stagger,
Dry the beads of fear which stand out on your plum cheeks,
Dry your tears
And think about your mother.

Think about your mother
In the evening, at bedtime;
Think about your mother
In the morning
When the light is born again.

Think about the one who, with her agile fingers
Weaved your black hair
And your arched eyebrows...

Child
Little child,
Wherever you are,
Think about your mother.

Zadi Zaourou (Côte d'Ivoire)

Voices

They speak of taxes
Of oil and power

They speak of honour
And pride of tribe

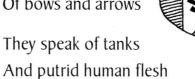

They speak of war
Of bows and arrows

They speak of tanks
And putrid human flesh

I sing my love
For Maria.

Ken Saro-Wiwa (Nigeria)

Lullaby

Someone would like to have you for her child
but you are mine.
Someone would like to rear you on a costly mat
but you are mine.
Someone would like to place you on a camel blanket
but you are mine.
I have you to rear on a torn old mat.
Someone would like to have you as her child
but you are mine.

Traditional, Akan (Ghana/Côte d'Ivoire)

Friendship

Friendship
Is precious
Keep it
Protect it
You will need it
Don't throw it away
Don't break it
Don't neglect it
Keep it
Somewhere
In your heart
If you want to
Somewhere in your thoughts
If you want to
But keep it
For, friendship
Has no borders
And its boundary
Is that of the world
It is the colour
Of the rainbow
And it has the beauty
Of a dream

Never listen
To those who say
It doesn't exist any more
It is here
It is yours
When you want it
All you have to do is:
Open
Your eyes

Véronique Tadjo (Côte d'ivoire)

The Heart Stays Young

The body perishes, the heart stays young.
The platter wears away with serving food.
No log retains its bark when old,
No lover peaceful while the rival weeps.

Traditional, Zulu (South Africa)

Extract from

My Life is a Song

At times, people ask me where I come from
And I reply: 'I don't know
For a long time, I have been on the path
That takes me here.
But I know I was born of the love
Between the earth and the sun'

My whole life is a song
I sing to say how much I love you
My whole life is a song
I hum next to you.

This evening, it rained. The road is wet
But I want to stay with you and take you to the country where
I come from
Where my secret is hidden.
And you, too, will be born of the love
Between the earth and the sun.

My whole life is a song
I sing to say how much I love you
My whole life is a song
I hum next to you.

Francis Bebey (Cameroon)

Quicksand

Playfully you took my hand
I felt free
To run with you
In the fields
Of red sand
And did not see
The rich red earth
Turn into deadly dunes
Beyond the desert

Now
My feet once so resolute and firm
Have fallen out of step
Defenceless
In my leap to your land
In your lethal quicksand
I can only sink
      sink
      sink

Playfully you took my hand
I felt free
To run with you
In the fields
Of red sand
And did not see
The rich red earth
Turn into deadly dunes
Beyond the desert

Irene Assiba D'Almeida (Benin Republic)

The Drum

Do you know the language of the drum?
The drum of celebrations,
The drum which summons spirits.
The drum of the wrestler dripping with sweat.
The drum of death.
Do you know the language of the drum?
It is the secret of the forest.

Fatou Ndiaye Sow (Senegal)

What a Fool he is!

When I asked for him at Entoto, he was towards Akaki,
So they told me;
When I asked for him at Akaki, he was towards Jarer,
So they told me;
When I asked for him at Jarer, he was at Mendar,
So they told me;
When I asked for him at Mendar, he was towards Awash,
So they told me;
When I asked for him at Awash, he was towards Chercher,
So they told me;
When I asked for him at Chercher, he was towards Harar,
So they told me;
When I asked for him at Harar, he was towards Djibouti,
So they told me;
When I asked for him at Djibouti, he had crossed the sea,
Or so they said:
I sent to find him a hundred times,
But I never found him.
I sit by the fire and weep:
What a fool he is
To hope he will ever find anyone to equal me.

Traditional, Amhara (Ethiopia)

Extract from

When You go to Dance

When you go to dance
You adorn yourself for the dance,
If your string-skirt
Is ochre-red
You do your hair
With ochre,
And you smear your body
With red oil
And you are beautifully red all over!
If you put on a black string-skirt
You do your hair with akuku
Your body shines with simsim oil
And the tattoos on your chest
And on your back
Glitter in the evening sun.
And the healthy sweat
On your bosom
Is like the glassy fruits of ocuga.

Okot p'Bitek (Uganda)

Girl's Song for the Game of 'Pots'

Leader:
We mould a pot as our mothers did.
The pot, where is the pot?

Chorus:
The pot it is here.
We mould the pot as our mothers did.
First, the base of the pot.

Leader:
Strip by strip and layer by layer,
Supple fingers kneading the clay,
Long fingers moulding the clay,
Stiff thumbs shaping the clay,
Layer by layer and strip by strip,
We build up the pot of our mother.

Chorus:
We build up the pot of our mother,
Strip by strip and layer by layer.
Its belly swells like the paunch of a hyena,
Its belly swells like a mother of twins.
It is a beautiful pot, the pot of our mother.
It swells like a mother of twins.

Leader:

Oh, clay of the river, bend to our hands,

Curve delicately,

See the strong shoulder and narrow neck.

(In, children, in)

Strip by strip and layer by layer,

Supple fingers kneading,

Long fingers moulding,

Stiff thumbs shaping,

The beautiful pot, the pot of our mother.

All:

The pot, the pot of our mother.

Traditional, Didinga (Uganda)

Awakening & Initiations

Love's always the starting point
Till the season insists on corpses,
On memories of the dead...
But life re-affirms itself in new
beginnings;
And suddenly, it is morning again!

And the stories we tell,
Of our meeting, and parting,
And returning,
Are

Minted coins...

Okinba Launko (Nigeria)

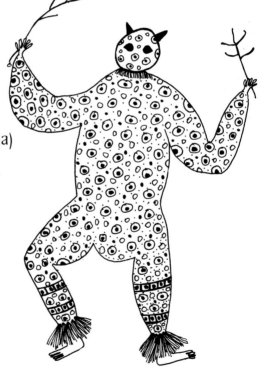

People

Praise Song to King Shaka

The nations he hath all destroyed,
Whither shall he now attack?
He! Whither shall he now attack?
He defeated kings,
Whither shall he now attack?
The nations he hath all destroyed,
Whither shall he now attack?
He! He! He! Whither shall he now attack?

Traditional, Zulu (South Africa)

Extract from

Is the Chief Greater than the Hunter?

Is the chief greater than the hunter?
  Arrogance! Hunter? Arrogance!
The pair of beautiful things on your feet,
The sandals that you wear,
How did it all happen?
It is the hunter that killed the duyker.

Does the chief say he is greater than the hunter?
  Arrogance! Hunter? Arrogance!

Traditional, Akan (Ghana)

Lazybones

Lazybones, let's go to the farm
  Sorry, I've got a headache
Lazybones, let's go pounding grain
  Sorry, my leg isn't right
Lazybones, let's go fetch firewood
  Sorry, my hands are hurting
Lazybones, come and have some food
  Hold on, let me wash my hands!

Traditional (Malawi)

Who are You?

Who are you?
I am Mamadi, son of Diabate.
Where do you come from?
I come from my village.
Where are you going?
To the other village.
Which village?
What does it matter?
I go wherever there are people.

What do you do in life?

I am a griot, do you understand?
I am a griot like my father was
Like the father of my father was
Like my children will be
And the children of my children.

I am a griot who lives like in the old times
Of the fires of joy and ritual dances
To sing the heroic deeds of the valiant warrior
And the kindness of the rich man
Who lets his honey spill over into my calabash
And his millet scatter on the floor of my hut.

I am a griot, do you understand?
I am a griot like in my father's time
When they welcomed the day being born
And gave hospitality to the unknown traveller
Caught up on the road of the night
I am a descendant of Dieli,
The man whose brother gave
His own flesh and his own blood
To save him from a terrible hunger
Dressed on the burning path of the forest
Like the menacing mask of the skeleton of death.

I am a child of Guinea,
I am a son of Mali,
I come from Tchad or far away Benin,
I am a child of Africa...
I wear a big white boubou
And white people laugh when they see me
Scurrying about barefoot on the dusty path...

They laugh?
Let them have a good laugh.
As for me, I clap my hands and the great sun of Africa
Stops in the Zenith to look and listen to me,
And I sing, and I dance
And I sing, and I dance.

Francis Bebey (Cameroon)

Nomadic Poem

my tree the aloe plant
my flower the crack in the cactus
my river there is none in my country
my basaltic universe in the desert
my close circle of camels
my weapon the dagger
my shadow is lanky
survival is my main
endeavour
my scenery the unchanging horizon
the dust stirred up by my soles of sheep's hide
the territory always
in front of me
my guide the desert
my book the sky
every evening picked up
my speech each stone
each flint
my dream always the same:
the nomadic child,
in the simplest state of being

Abdourahman A. Waberi (Djibouti)

Shores of my Childhood

Shores of my childhood
Distant shores
Ephemeral smiles from afar
I think back to the smoky warmth of hearts
That light up
In the smoke-filled huts
I remember the freshness of faces
Over the clear waters
Of the river of yesterday
Which slowly disapear
Like children's dreams.
If the heart cries at cockcrow
the mind will catch fire before long

Hamidou Dia (Senegal)

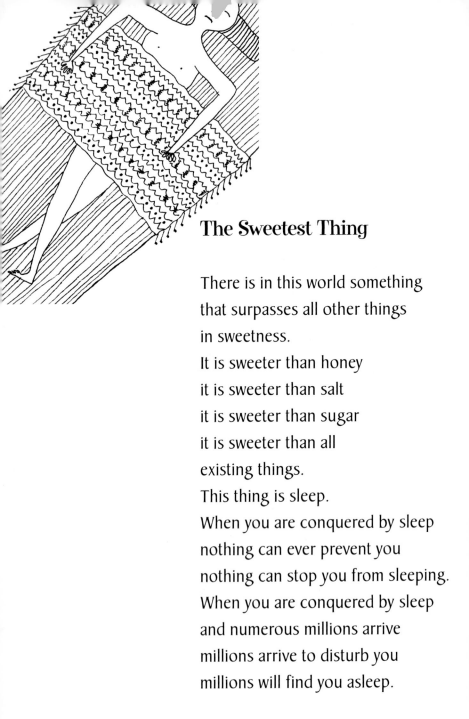

The Sweetest Thing

There is in this world something
that surpasses all other things
in sweetness.
It is sweeter than honey
it is sweeter than salt
it is sweeter than sugar
it is sweeter than all
existing things.
This thing is sleep.
When you are conquered by sleep
nothing can ever prevent you
nothing can stop you from sleeping.
When you are conquered by sleep
and numerous millions arrive
millions arrive to disturb you
millions will find you asleep.

Traditional, Soussou

Extract from

When the Cock Crows

When the cock crows,
the lazy man smacks his lips and says:
So it is daylight again is it?
And before he turns over heavily,
before he even stretches himself,
before he even yawns –
the farmer has reached the farm,
the water carriers arrived at the river,
the spinners are spinning their cotton,
the weaver works on his cloth,
and the fire blazes in the blacksmith's hut.

Traditional, Yoruba (Nigeria)

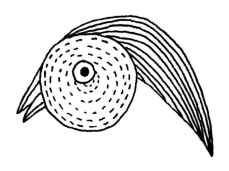

Song of the Stranger Come to Stay

For the stranger his first day
Rice and flying-fish provide,
Hug him, welcome him inside,
Stranger who has come to stay.

On the stranger's second day
Give him milk and butter too.
Let love greatly grow in you,
For the stranger come to stay.

Stranger now on his third day,
Three cups of rice is all we've got
Left for food. Cook, eat the lot
With the stranger come to stay.

Stranger now on his fourth day,
Send him off to help them hoe.
When he comes back bid him go
Home, dear stranger come to stay.

Look at stranger his fifth day,
Thin as needle he has gone.
Gossip now goes on and on
'Bout the stranger come to stay.

Stranger on the sixth long day,
When you eat he mustn't know,
In some hidden corner go,
Hide from stranger come to stay.

Stranger on the seventh day –
Someone set the roof alight.
Guilty man is known all right,
That's the monster come to stay.

Tell the stranger his eighth day,
Just come in a moment, then
Say when he goes out again,
Goodbye, stranger come to stay.

Tell the stranger his ninth day,
Go in peace, my son, but go,
Only don't come back, you know,
Go, you stranger come to stay.

Stranger now on his tenth day,
Chuck him out with kick and clout!
Chuck him, chuck him, chuck him
    Out!
Out, you stranger come to stay!

Traditional, Swahili (Kenya, Tanzania)

The European

In the blue palace of the deep ocean
dwells a strange being.
His skin is white like salt
his hair long like plaited seaweed.
His dress is made of fishes,
fishes more charming than birds.
His house is built of brass rods
his garden is a forest of tobacco leaves.
His country is strewn with white pearls
like sand on the beach.

Traditional, Gamma

The Poor Man

The poor man knows not how to eat with the rich man.
when they eat fish, he eats the head.

Invite a poor man and he rushes in
licking his lips and upsetting the plates.

The poor man has no manners, he comes along
with the blood of lice under his nails.

The face of the poor man is lined
From the hunger and thirst in his belly.

Poverty is no state for any mortal man.
It makes him a beast to be fed on grass.

Poverty is unjust. If it befalls a man,
Though he is nobly born, he has no power with God.

Traditional, Swahili (Kenya/Tanzania)

Life's Variety

Why do we grumble because a tree is bent,
When, in our streets, there are even men who are bent?
Why must we complain that the new moon is slanting?
Can anyone reach the skies to straighten it?
Can't we see that some cocks have combs on their heads but
no plumes
in their tails?
And some have plumes in their tails, but no claws on their
toes?
And others have claws on their toes, but no power to crow?
He who has a head has no cap to wear, and he who has a cap
has no head
to wear it on.
The Owa has everything but a horse's stable.
Some great scholars of Ifa cannot tell the way to Ofa.
Others know the way to Ofa, but not one line of Ifa.
Great eaters have no food to eat, and great drinkers no
 wine to drink:
Wealth has a coat of many colours.

Traditional, Yoruba (Nigeria)

Extract from

I Love my Matatu

This is my matatu
and i love my matatu

i shall fill it with
stacks of human beings
to the brim
i shall make more money
enough to pay for
the matatu loan
the matatu insurance
the profit...
not to mention my
official and non official pay

my matatu never gets full
there is always space
for one more
we all travel seated standing, kneeling and
bottoms up

the fat travellers have a tendency
to take up much more space
remind me to leave them out
next time
tell them to take the bus

Cecilia Muhoho (Kenya)

One Small Boy Longs for Summer

We can't play outside – I must not go, I know
      How we danced in the rain. We are so tired
Of the winter: it's so dingy outside.
We can't play inside – I'm so tied up.
It's so boring, I feel like bursting into
A cracking laughter; but father,
He'll go mad.
It's so steamy inside
I feel I could bite the walls down.
If only it makes the winter pass.

M. Pascal Gwala (South Africa)

Death

Death

Death is when one is very old
then one lies down one evening
and one cannot wake up any more
The sleeping man is carried to a village
where everybody sleeps all the time
Each one of them alone in a bed
dug in the earth

Ahmed Tidjani Cissé (Guinea)

Refugee Mother and Child

No Madonna and Child could touch
that picture of a mother's tenderness
for a son she soon would have to forget.

The air was heavy with odours
of diarrhoea of unwashed children
with washed-out ribs and dried up
Bottoms struggling in laboured
steps behind blown empty bellies. Most
mothers there had long ceased
to care but not this one; she held
a ghost smile between her teeth
and in her eyes the ghost of a mother's
pride as she combed the rust-coloured
hair left on his skull and then –
singing in her eyes – began carefully
to part it ... In another life this
would have been a little daily
act of no consequence before his
breakfast and school; now she
did it like putting flowers
on a tiny grave.

Chinua Achebe (Nigeria)

When I Die

There is no needle without piercing point.
There is no razor without trenchant blade.
Death comes to us in many forms.

With our feet we walk the goat's earth.
With our hands we touch God's sky.
Some future day in the heat of noon,
I shall be carried shoulder high
through the village of the dead.
When I die, don't bury me under forest trees,
I fear their thorns.
When I die, don't bury me under forest trees.
I fear the dripping water.
Bury me under the great shade trees in the market,
I want to hear the drums beating
I want to feel the dancers' feet.

Traditional, Kuba

Extract from

Breath

Listen more to things
Than to words that are said
The water's voice sings
And the flame cries
And the wind that brings
The woods to sighs
Is the breathing of the dead.

Those who are dead have never gone away.
They are in the shadows darkening around,
They are in the shadows fading into day,
The dead are not under the ground.
They are in the trees that quiver,
They are in the woods that weep,
They are in the waters of the rivers,
They are in the waters that sleep.
They are in the crowds, they are in the homestead.
The dead are never dead.

Listen more to things
Than to words that are said.
The water's voice sings
And the flame cries
And the wind that brings
The woods to sighs
Is the breathing of the dead.
Who have not gone away
Who are not under the ground
Who are never dead.

Birago Diop (Senegal)

Value

It is Man who matters.
I call God:
It is silent.
I call cloth:
It is silent.
It is Man who matters.

Traditional, Akan (Ghana/Côte d'Ivoire)

Bang!

Bang! I shall kill Death. Bang!
There was a man who said:
I shall kill Death. Bang!
She will never be able to come close to me;
I shall live surrounded by a thousand doctors.
Bang! Death started by making all the doctors ill.

Bang! I shall kill Death. Bang!
There was an ant who said:
I shall kill Death.
I shall make myself even smaller,
So she will not see me anymore.
Bang! Death turned herself into an ant-eater.

Bang! I shall kill Death. Bang!
There was a man who said:
Bang! I shall kill Death. Bang!
The best solution is to be heartless.
I shall kill everything around me.
Bang! Death crushed him under the weight of loneliness.

Bang! I shall kill Death. Bang!
There was a tree who said:
I shall kill Death. Bang!
I shall keep growing.
She won't be able to touch my head.
Bang! Death made him burn his head in the sun.

Bang! I shall kill death. Bang!
Now, it is a Zebra who says:
I shall kill Death. Bang!
I am fast, very fast.
She will never catch up with me.
Bang! Wait till Death hears him...

Williams Sassine (Guinea)

Pride and Defiance

Young Africa's Lament

I am half starved;
I asked for bread they gave me stone.
I am thirsty;
I asked for water they gave me slush.
They tell the horse to wait awhile
Because green grasses would soon grow
And dry Sahara would yield great streams.

Dennis Chukude Osadebay (Nigeria)

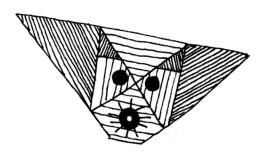

Extract from

Prayer to Masks

Masks! Masks!

Black mask, red mask, you white-and-black masks

Masks of the four points from which the Spirit blows

In silence I salute you!

Nor you the least, the Lion-headed Ancestor

You guard this place forbidden to all laughter of women, to
all smiles that fade

You distil this air of eternity in which I breathe the air of
my fathers.

Masks of unmasked faces, stripped of the marks of illness
and the lines of age

You have fashioned this portrait, this my face bent
over the altar of white paper

In your own image, hear me!

Léopold Sédar Senghor (Senegal)

I Thank You God

I thank you God for creating me black,
For making of me
Porter of all sorrows,
Setting on my head
The World.
I wear the Centaur's hide
And I have carried the World since the first morning.

White is the colour for special occasions
Black the colour for every day
And I have carried the World since the first evening.

I am glad
Of the shape of my head
Made to carry the World,
Content
With the shape of my nose
That must snuff every wind of the World
Pleased
With the shape of my legs
Ready to run all the heats of the World.

I thank you God for creating me black
For making of me
Porter of all sorrows.

Thirty-six swords have pierced my heart.
Thirty-six fires have burnt my body.
And my blood on all calvaries has reddened the snow,
And my blood at every dawn has reddened all nature.

Still I am
Glad to carry the World,
Glad of my short arms
   of my long arms
      of the thickness of my lips.

I thank you God for creating me black.
White is a colour for special occasions
Black the colour for every day
And I have carried the World since the dawn of time.
And my laugh over the World, through the night creates the
Day.

I thank you God for creating me black.

Bernard Dadié (Côte d'Ivoire)

Extract from

Africa

Africa my Africa
Africa of proud warriors in ancestral savannahs
Africa of whom my grandmother sings
On the banks of the distant river
I have never known you
But your blood flows in my veins
Your beautiful black blood that irrigates the fields
The blood of your sweat
The sweat of your work
The work of your slavery
The slavery of your children
Africa tell me Africa
Is this your back that is bent
This back that breaks under the weight of humiliation
This back trembling with red scars
And saying yes to the whip under the midday sun?

But a grave voice answers me
Impetuous child that tree young and strong
That tree over there
Splendidly alone amidst white and faded flowers
That is your Africa springing up anew
Springing up patiently obstinately
Whose fruits bit by bit acquire
The bitter taste of liberty.

David Diop (Senegal)

Defiance against Force

You, bowing, you, crying
You, dying, like that, one day without knowing why
You, struggling, you watching over another's rest
You looking no longer with laughter in your eyes
You, my brother, your face full of fear and suffering
Stand up and shout NO!

David Diop (Senegal)

The One Who Has Lost Everything

The sun shone in my hut
And my wives were beautiful and supple
Like palm trees in the evening breeze.
My children slid on the great river
As deep as Death.
And my canoes fought with crocodiles.
The moon like a mother watched over our dances.
The fast and heavy rhythm of the drum,
Drum of joy, drum of carefree life
    In the midst of the fires of freedom.

Then one day, Silence...
The rays of the sun seemed to go out
In my hut emptied of meaning.
My wives crushed their reddened mouths
Against the thin hard lips of the conquerors with eyes of
steel
And my children left their peaceful nudity
For the uniform of iron and blood.
Your voice has gone out, too
The irons of slavery have torn my heart apart
Drums of my nights, drums of my fathers.

David Diop (Senegal)

Extract from

Dry Your Tears, Africa!

Dry your tears, Africa!
Your children come back to you
their hands full of presents
and their hearts full of love.
They return to clothe you
in their dreams and their hopes.

Bernard Dadié (Côte d'Ivoire)

The Changing Times

Conflict

Here we stand
infants overblown,
poised between two civilisations,
finding the balance irksome,
itching for something to happen,
to tip us one way or the other,
groping in the dark for a helping hand
and finding none.
I'm tired, O my God, I'm tired,
I'm tired of hanging in the middle way –
but where can I go?

Mabel Segun (Nigeria)

Western Civilization

Sheets of tin nailed to posts
driven in the ground
make up the house.

Some rags complete
the intimate landscape.

The sun slanting through cracks
welcomes the owner

After twelve hours of slave labour.

breaking rock
shifting rock
breaking rock
shifting rock
fair weather
wet weather
breaking rock
shifting rock

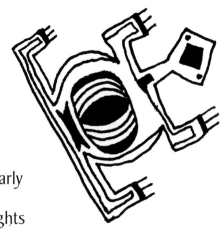

Old age comes early

a mat on dark nights
is enough when he dies
gratefully
of hunger.

Agostinho Neto (Angola)

Extract from

City Johannesburg

This way I salute you;
My hand pulses to my back trouser pocket
Or into my inner jacket pocket
For my pass, my life,
Jo'burg City.
My hand like a starved snake rears my pockets
For my thin, ever lean wallet,
While my stomach groans a friendly smile to hunger
Jo'burg City
My stomach also devours coppers and papers
Don't you know?
Jo'burg City, I salute you;
When I run out, or roar in a bus to you,
I leave behind me, my love –
My comic houses and people, my donga and my ever
                                        Whirling dust.

Mongane Wally Serote (South Africa)

The Song of Life

Time passes
The sun
Burns the land
And brings about anxiety
But one day
The rainy season
Arrives
And the trees start burgeoning
The mango trees
The lemon trees
The guava trees
Give out their scents
The hibiscus flowers
Show off their beauty
The flame trees
Dance in the wind
And the whole savannah
Sings
And people
Dance
And the Mask
Dances
And the tom-tom
Beats the cadence
Of life
Which comes back

Again and again
For, people die
And people are born
People die
And people are born
Until the end
Of time.

Véronique Tadjo (Cote d'Ivoire)

Extract from
I Write for a New Dawn

I write for the new dawn
A poem of flowers and suns
I write for my country in ruins
Whose proud mountains
Light up the morning
That came out from the abyss of the night
I write for the man
Whose cry shatters the horizon
Of my prison-like hemisphere.

Paul Dakeyo (Cameroon)

Extract from

Who Knows the Country Where I Come From?

who knows the country where I come from
this country of stupor
landmarked by red flesh
this country of bizarre decrees
this country of deep wounds and abysmal tears
who knows
the whipping that I have endured
the humiliation I have drunk
who knows
the prayers that I have said
the hatred that I had to confess
the loves which have left me desperate
the winters which my soul has suffered
who knows the country where I come from
the bitter country of the anaconda like charlatans
you who know of this country
raise with me
the battalion of the valiant hearts
the battalions of hope

N. X. Ebony (Côte d'Ivoire)

End of the War

They say,
A war only ends, when
Another war begins:

The silence of the battlefield
Heralds the widow's anguish

For, to set questions
Is not as hard as finding answers…

Our war has ended
Because war is now with us

The deserted houses, the fallen rafters
Breed the city's slums
And the praise-singers are not dead
They have only gone to the barracks…
The butchers fill the parliaments…
And the victims no longer die by bullets
But survive to pay the levies…

Listen – they will tell you –
To beat drums is mere children's play
The adult's is to start echoes…

Okinba Launko (Nigeria)

Extract from

Why Am I So Cynical About My Country Now?

Why, why am I so
Cynical about my country now?
God make me love my country again
It is the only one I have
I have no other
I cannot live anywhere else
I can travel to the East or West
For weeks or months
As the case may be
But I always long to return
To my country
In spite of all the attractions
Of foreign lands, where things
Are orderly,
Where everything works
How, how can one be comfortable
In a country that is not one's own?

Flora Nwapa (Nigeria)

And Because...

And because we have too much information,
And no clear direction,
Too many facts,
And not enough faith,
Too much confusion,
And crave clear vision;
Too many fears,
And not enough light –
I whisper to myself modest maxims
As thought-friends for a new age.
   See clearly, think clearly.
   Face pleasant and unpleasant truths;
   Face reality.
   Free the past.
   Catch up with ourselves.
   Never cease from upward striving.
   We are better than we think.
   Don't be afraid to love, or be loved.
   As within, so without.
   We owe life abundant happiness.

Ben Okri (Nigeria)

Telephone Conversation

The price seemed reasonable, location
Indifferent. The landlady swore she lived
Off premises. Nothing remained
But self-confession. 'Madam,' I warned,
'I hate a wasted journey – I am African.'
Silence. Silenced transmission of
Pressurized good-breeding. Voice, when it came,
Lipstick coated, long gold-rolled
Cigarette-holder pipped. Caught I was, foully.
'HOW DARK?'... I had not misheard... 'ARE YOU LIGHT
OR VERY DARK?' Button B. Button A. Stench
Of rancid breath of public hide-and-speak.
Red booth. Red pillar-box. Red double-tiered
Omnibus squelching tar. It was real! Shamed
By ill-mannered silence, surrender
Pushed dumbfoundment to beg simplification.
Considerate she was, varying the emphasis –
'ARE YOU DARK? OR VERY LIGHT?' Revelation came.
'You mean – like plain or milk chocolate?'
Her accent was clinical, crushing in its light
Impersonality. Rapidly, wave-length adjusted,
I chose. 'West African sepia' – and as afterthought,
'Down in my passport.' Silence for spectroscopic
Flight of fancy, till truthfulness changed her accent
Hard on the mouthpiece. 'WHAT'S THAT?' conceding

'DON'T KNOW WHAT THAT IS.' 'Like brunette.'
'THAT'S DARK, ISN'T IT,' 'Not altogether.
Facially, I am brunette, but madam, you should see
The rest of me. Palm of my hand, soles of my feet
Are a peroxide blonde. Friction, caused –
Foolishly madam – by sitting down, has turned
My bottom raven black – One moment madam! – sensing
Her receiver rearing on the thunderclap
About my ears – 'Madam,' I pleaded, 'wouldn't you rather
See for yourself?'

Wole Soyinka (Nigeria)

In my Country

In my country they jail you
For what they think you think.
My uncle once said to me:
They'll implant a microchip
In our minds
To flash our thoughts and dreams
On to a screen at John Vorster Square.
I was scared:
By day I guard my tongue
By night my dreams.

Pitika Ntuli (South Africa)

I Have Come to Look for a Job

I have come to look for a job.
I hope I'll get one.
I have come from my far-away home
To find work in your country.

I have left everything, my wife, my friends
Over there at home
I hope I'll find them all alive
The day I return.

My poor mother was very sad
When she saw me leaving
I told her I'll come back one day
To end her misery

I have done many long days of travelling
To come all the way here
Was I not assured of a welcome
Well worth that suffering?

Look at me, I am tired
Of being on the road
I haven't eaten anything for days
Could you spare a bit of bread?

My trousers are all torn
But I don't have any other pair
Don't yell, it is not outrageous
I am only poor.

I have come to look for a job
I hope I'll get one
I have come from my far-away home
To find work in your country.

Francis Bebey (Cameroon)

Extracts from
Exile
III

another immigrant's question:
'Where were you born?'

I
was born in africa
free happy hopeful
once upon a time
proud presumptuous fanciful
once upon a time

I
was born in the cradle of the world's culture
the roots of the human race
the maker of marvellous myths
a continent of many many countries
another question:
'Where exactly were you born?'

I
was born in an african country
causing me shame
making me mad and sad
a life-threatening cancer
a symbol of death pulling the plug on innocent lives
a monster from whom we all wish to flee
forever

IV
exile
is
a long night waiting for a miraculous dawn in your faraway
home walking
the streets of a strange land in search of your family and
   friends
seeking desperately to fathom the soul of civilization's com-
puterized society

exile
is
living in a halfway house on the highway between heaven
and hell feeling
fat but feeling forever empty shouting but hardly making a
sound

exile
is
having a house but not a home
having a choice to go somewhere but with nowhere to go
wanting
to go home but not daring to go home

exile
is
heaven
      and
      hell

Femi Ojo-Ade (Nigeria)

Afro-German

You're Afro-German?
...oh, I see: African and German.
An interesting mixture!
You know, there are people who still think
   Mulattos won't get
   As far in life
   As whites

I don't believe that
I mean: given the same type of education...
   You're pretty lucky to have grown up here.
   With German parents, even. Think of that!

Do you want to go back some day?
What, you've never been to your Dad's country?
   That's so sad... Listen, if you ask me:
A person's origin, see, leaves quite a mark.
Take me, I'm from Westfalia,
And I feel
That's where I belong...

Oh, boy! All the misery there is in the world!
   Be glad
   You don't still live in the bush.
   You wouldn't be where you are today!

I mean, you're really quite an intelligent girl, you know.
   If you work hard at your studies,
   You can help your people in Africa: That's
    What you're predestined to do;
    I'm sure they'd listen to you,
Whereas people like us –
There's such a difference in cultural levels...

What do you mean, do something here? What would you
want to do here?
OK, OK, so it's not all sunshine. But I think
   Everyone should put their own house in order first!

May Opitz (Afro-German)

None so Blind

They were looking at me
But they did not see me;
They thought they saw me
But what they saw
Was not the real ME –
The ME that yearned for perfection,
The ME that wept for redemption
From all the ills
That plagued that
Which I love most;
The ME that dreamt about glory –
The glory that could be
If only THEY were less greedy;
The glory that could be
If only THEY were less selfish;
The glory that could be
If only THEY were more honest
And sincere in their proclamations.
But, no, they did not see that ME;
All they saw was the me that stood
Between them and their ambitions –

The Impossible me!
The Adamant me!
The Militant me!
The Too Rigid me!
The – oh, I could go on –
They saw only the shadow
Of the real ME
They did not see ME at all
They did not WANT to see
The REAL ME.

Mabel Segun (Nigeria)

Map

Senegal
Gambia
Guinea-Bissau
Guinea
Sierra Leone
Liberia
Côte d'Ivoire
Mali
Niger
Burkina Faso
Nigeria
Ghana
Togo
Benin
Gabon
Cameroon
Chad
Sudan
Central African Republic
Congo
Democratic Republic of Congo
Eritrea
Djibouti
Ethiopa
Somalia
Uganda
Kenya
Rwanda
Burundi
Malawi
Angola
Zambia
Namibia
Mozambique
Madagascar
Botswana
South Africa
Lesotho
Swaziland
Zimbabwe

Poets

Angola
Agostinho Neto (1922-79)
Western Civilization, p.72

Benin Republic
Irene Assiba d'Almeida (birthdate not obtainable)
Crab, p.23; *Quicksand*, p.33

Burundi
Traditional
A Heart, p 26

Cameroon
Francis Bebey (b.1929)
My Life is a Song, p.32;
Who are You? p.42;
I Have Come to Look for a Job, p.82
Paul Dakeyo (b.1948)
I Write for a New Dawn, p.75
Claude-Joseph M'bafou-Zetebeg (b.1948)
The Free Bird, p.24
Traditional
Invocation to the Rainbow, p.8

Côte d'Ivoire
Bernard Dadié (b.1916)
I Thank You God, p.64;
Dry Your Tears, Africa!, p.70
N.X. Ebony (1944-86)
Who Knows the Country Where I Come From? p.76
Veronique Tadjo (b.1955)
Friendship, p.30,
The Song of Life, p.74
Zadi Zaourou (b.1939)
As Soon as Night Falls, p.27

Djibouti
Abdourahman A. Waberi (b.1965)
Nomadic Poem, p.44

Ethiopia
Traditional
What a Fool he is, p35

Gabon
Traditional
Invocation to the Rainbow, p.8

Ghana
Abena P. A. Busia (b.1953)
Mawu of the Waters, p.11
Traditional
Is the Chief Greater than the Hunter? p.41

Guinea
Ahmed Tidjani Cisse (b.1941)
Death, p.55
Williams Sassine (1944-97)
Bang! p.60

Kenya
Cecilia Muhoho (b.1963)
I Love my Matatu, p.53

Malawi
Traditional
Lazybones, p.41

Nigeria
Chinua Achebe (b.1930)
Refugee Mother and Child, p.56
Okinba Launko (b.1946)
Awakening & Inititations, p.39;
End of the War, p.77
Flora Nwapa (b.1931)
Why am I so Cynical About My Country Now?, p.78
Uzo Nwokedi (b.1962)
The Lion, p.15
Femi Ojo-Ade (b.1943)
Exile, p.84
Ben Okri (b.1959)
And Because..., p.79
Dennis Chukude Osadebay (1911-95)
Young Africa's Lament, p.62
Niyi Osundare (b.1947)
But Sometimes When it Rains, p.12;
A Baby Antelope, p.18
Ken Saro-Wiwa (1941-95)
Voices, p.29

Glossary

akuku   traditional hair treatment
boubou   a very ample traditional gown worn by men and women alike, but in different styles
calabash   a fruit which is dried and used as a container for liquids or grain
donga   a shanty house
duyker   a very small antelope that lives in the bush or grasslands
Elmina, and
Cape Coast   places in Ghana
griots   singers, story-tellers, poets and historians generally attached to kings and notables. Griots had a hereditary special status in traditional society.
hornbill   a big and beautiful bird that lives in the forest. It has a large bill and horny growths on its head.
Hunter   'the Hunter above' is God – an image used by the hunter to portray the supreme being as the most important hunter of all!
Ifa   traditional religion of the Yoroba; also the name of the religion's sacred text
kob antelope   a deer-sized antelope with s-shaped horns
'lion-headed
ancestor'   an ancestor whose spirit is as noble and strong as that of a lion's.
Mamadu   son of Diabate – both griots
The Mask   a sacred carving worn over the face of a dancer whose identity is secret. It represents a spirit, an ancestor or a mythical animal. A mask is worn only by a specially chosen person, who leads the villagers in their dance. There is music and singing to accompany the mask wherever it leads. Masks in Africa are considered by many to be the symbols of traditional African spirituality.
matatu   a mini-bus used for public transport and usually overloaded with passengers.
Mawu   the goddess of water
ochre-red   a yellowish-red pigment
ocuga   a fruit
Ofa   A Yoruba town
Owa   a King
Shaka (King)   powerful Zulu king from South Africa who resisted British invasion.
simsim oil   oil used by women on their bodies
string skirt   raffia skirt, sometimes dyed

Index of first lines

Acknowledgements

We are grateful to the following for permission to reproduce copyright material:

Irène Assiba d'Almeida for her poems 'Crab' and 'Quicksand'. **Abena P. A. Busia** for her poem 'Mawu of the Waters'. **CEDA - Abidjan** for 'As Soon as Night Falls' by Bernard Zadi Zaourou and 'Friendship', The Song of Life' by Véronique Tadjo. **Ad Donker Publishers** for 'City Johannesburg' from *Selected Poems*, Mongane Wally Serote, Ad Donker Publishers 1982. **East African Educational Publishers Ltd.** for 'Western Civilisation' by Agostinho Neto, translated from the Portuguese by Margaret Dickinson and for 'When you go to dance' by Okot p'Bitek. **Editions Nouvelles du Sud** for 'I Write for a New Dawn' by Paul Dakeyo, translated from the French by Véronique Tadjo. **Faber & Faber** for 'Song of the Stranger come to Stay', 'Young Africa's Lament' and 'Praise Song to King Shaka' from *A History of Neo African Literature* by Janheinz Jahn. **Hatier** for 'The Free Bird' by Claude-Joseph M'Bafou-Zetebeg and 'I Have Come to Look for a Job' and 'My Life is a Song' by Francis Bebey, both translated from the French by Véronique Tadjo from *Anthologie africaine*, collection Monde Noir Poche, © Hatier. **Heinemann Educational Publishers**, a division of Reed Educational & Professional Publishing Ltd. for 'Refugee Mother and Child' by Chinua Achebe from *Beware Soul Brother*, Heinemann, Oxford 1979 and for 'On the Island' by Dennis Brutus from *A Simple Lust*, Heinemann, London, 1973. **Carole Machin** for 'Mother Parrot's Advice to her Children' by A.K. Nyabongo, 'Song of the Animal World' (Zaïre) Traditional, 'Love-song' (Soga) Traditional, 'Value' (Akan) Traditional and 'A heart' (Burundi) Traditional from African Poetry for Schools edited by Noel Machin, Longman, 1978. **Methuen Publishing Limited** for 'Telephone Conversation' by Wole Soyinka. **Cecilia Muhoho** for her poem 'I Love my Matutu'. **Les Nouvelles Editions Africaines du Sénégal** for 'Who Knows?' and 'The Key', by Fatou Ndiaye Sow, translated by Véronique Tadjo, 'The Drum' by Fatou Ndiaye Sow from *Takam-takam*, Les Nouvelles Editions Africaines, Dakar, 1981 and 'My House' by Annette Mbaye d'Ernville, translated by Véronique Tadjo, from *Chansons pour Laïty* Les Nouvelles Editions Africaines, Dakar, 1981. **Uzo Nwokedi** for her poem 'The Lion'. **Femi Ojo-Ade** for his poem 'Exile'. **Ben Okri** for his poem 'And Because...' from *Mental Fight* Phoenix House, London (1999) **Femi Osofisan** (Okinba Launko) for his poems 'End of the War' and 'Awakening & Initiations'. **Orlanda Berlin** for 'afro-deutsch!' ('Afro-German') from *blues in schwarz weiss*; 3rd ed, Orlanda Berlin, 1996; translated by George Busby. **Niyi Osundare** for his poems 'Baby Antelope' and 'But Sometimes When it Rains'. **Oxford University Press** for 'Prayer to Masks' by Léopold Sédar Senghor from *Léopold Sédar Senghor: Selected Poems* translated by John Reed and Clive Wake © Oxford University Press 1964. **Présence Africaine** for 'Breath' ('Souffles') by Birago Diop from *Leurres et lueurs*, Présence Africaine, 1960, 'The One who has Lost Everything' ('Celui qui a tout perdu'), 'Africa' ('Afrique') and 'Defiance against Force' ('Defi à la force) by David Diop from *Coups du Pilons*, Présence Africaine, 1973, 'Shores of My Childhood' ('Rivages de mon enface') by Hamidou Dia from *Les Remparts de la Mémoire*, Présence Africaine, 1999, 'Who are you?' ('Qui-es-tu?') by Francis Bebey from *Nouvelle somme de Poésie du Monde Noir, Revue Cuturelle Présence Africaine No57*, 1966, 'Bang!' ('Pan!') by Williams Sassine, extract from 'Le zébre' in *L'Alphabête*, Présence Africaine, 1982. **Mabel Segun** for her poems 'Conflict' and 'None so Blind' and 'The Lion Roars with a Fearful Sound'. **Véronique Tadjo** for her poem 'The Song of Life'. **Clive Wake and John Reed** for their translations of 'Souffles' ('Breath') by Birago Diop, 'Je vous remercie mon Dieu' ('I Thank You God') by Bernard Dadié, Défi à la force ('Defiance against force') by David Diop. **Abdourahman Waberi** for his poem 'Nomadic Poem', translated by Véronique Tadjo.

Every effort has been made to trace and acknowledge copyright, but in some cases copyright proved untraceable. If any right has been omitted, the publishers offer their apologies and will rectify this in subsequent editions.These poems have been previously published in the following anthologies (this list also includes traditional poems): 'Girl's Song for the game of 'Pots'' Traditional, Didinga (Uganda) and 'In My Country' by Pitika Ntuli from *Voices from Twentieth Century Africa*, Faber & Faber, 1988. 'One small boy longs for summer' by M Pascal Gwala from *Black Poets in South Africa*, Heinemann, 1978. 'Voices' by Ken Saro-Wiwa from *Songs in a time of war*, Saros International Publishers, 1985. 'Dry Your Tears, Africa!' by Bernard Dadié, 'What a fool he is!', Traditional from *The Heritage of African Poetry*, Longman 1985. 'Invocation to the Rainbow', Pygmy (Cameroon/Gabon) Traditional from *Anthologie de la poésie Negro-Africaine pour la jeunesse* edited by Anne-Marie Gey, NEA/Edicef, Paris 1986. 'What a fool he is!', Traditional, 'Is the Chief Greater than the Hunter?', Akan (Ghana) Traditional. 'The sky', Ewe (Ghana) Traditional and 'Life's variety', Yoruba (Nigeria) Traditional from *The Heritage of African Poetry*, Longman, 1985. 'Hymn to the Sun', Fang Traditional, 'Song of the Lioness for her Cub', hottentot Traditional, 'Kob Antelope', Yoruba Traditional, 'The Magnificent Bull', Dinka Traditional, 'Lullaby', Akan Traditional, 'Love', Zulu Traditional, 'The Sweetest Thing' ('The Heart Stays Young'), Soussou Traditional, 'The Lazy Man' ('When the Cock Crows'), Yoruruba Traditional 'The European' Gamma, Traditional, 'Death' ('When I Die'), Kuba Traditional, 'The Poor Man', Swahili Traditional from *African Poetry, an anthology of traditional African poems*, edited by Ulli Beier, Cambridge University Press, 1971. 'Death' by Ahmed Tidjani Cissé in *L'Afrique noire en poésie* edited by Pius Ngandu Nkashama and Bernard Magnier, Folio Junior, Paris 1986. 'Who knows the country where I come from?' by N X Ebony, from D.E.J.A. V.U. Editions Ouskokata Paris, 1983. 'Why am I so cynical about my country now?' by Flora Nwapa from *Cassava Song and Rice song*, Tana Press Ltd, 1986. 'Lazybones' Traditional (Malawi) from *Daughters of Africa*, Jonathan Cape, 1992.